The Circulatory System

by Helen Frost

Consulting Editor: Gail Saunders-Smith, Ph.D.

Consultant: Lawrence M. Ross, M.D., Ph.D.
Member, American Association of Clinical Anatomists

Pebble Books

an imprint of Capstone Press
Mankato, Minnesota

Pebble Books are published by Capstone Press
151 Good Counsel Drive, P.O. Box 669, Mankato, Minnesota 56002
http://www.capstone-press.com

1 2 3 4 5 6 06 05 04 03 02 01

Library of Congress Cataloging-in-Publication Data
Frost, Helen, 1949–
    The circulatory system/by Helen Frost.
    p. cm.—(Human body systems)
    Includes bibliographical references and index.
    Summary: Introduces the circulatory system, its purpose, parts, and functions.
    ISBN 0-7368-0648-2
    1. Cardiovascular system—Juvenile literature. [1. Circulatory system.] I. Title.
II. Human body systems (Mankato, Minn.)
QP103.F76 2001
612.1—dc21

                                          00-026996

Note to Parents and Teachers

The Human Body Systems series supports national science standards for units on understanding the basic functions of the human body. This book describes the circulatory system and illustrates its purpose, parts, and functions. The photographs and diagrams support early readers in understanding the text. This book also introduces early readers to subject-specific vocabulary words, which are defined in the Words to Know section. Early readers may need assistance to read some words and to use the Table of Contents, Words to Know, Read More, Internet Sites, and Index/Word List sections of the book.

Table of Contents

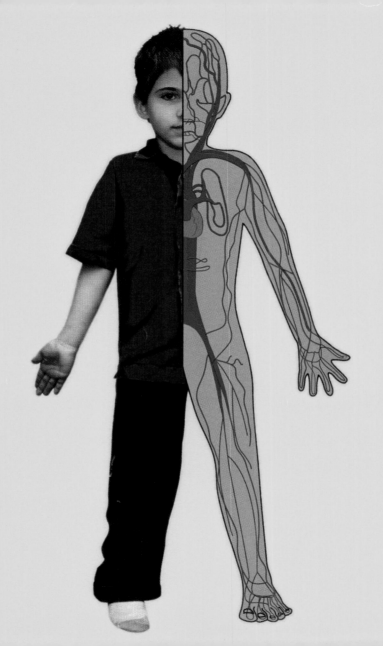

4

The circulatory system moves blood around the body. Blood helps keep the body healthy.

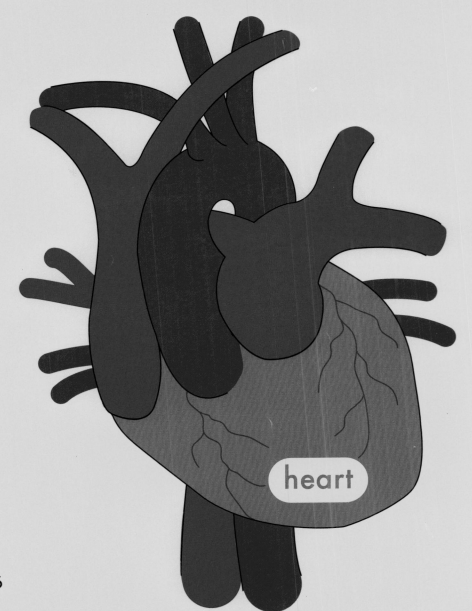

heart

The heart is a muscle that pumps blood through blood vessels. Blood vessels are thin tubes that carry blood to all parts of the body.

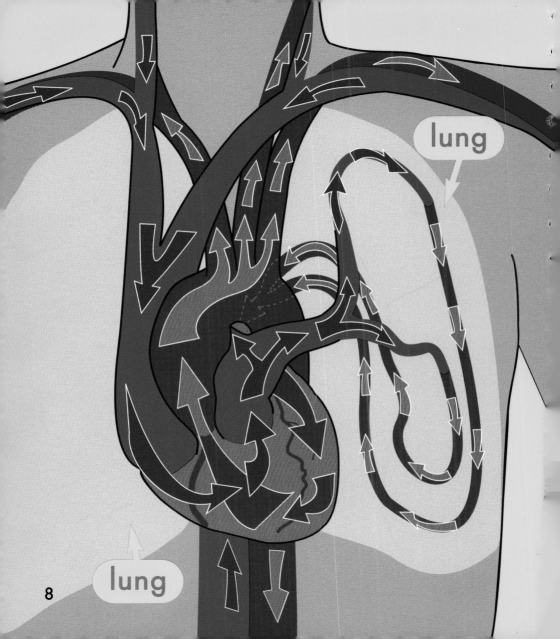

The heart pumps blood into the lungs. The blood picks up oxygen from the lungs. The blood then travels back into the heart.

The heart pumps the blood into the aorta. The aorta is an artery. Arteries are blood vessels that carry blood away from the heart.

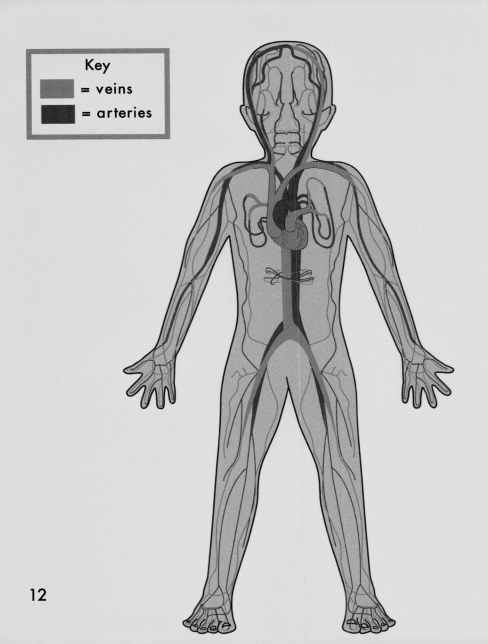

Key
= veins
= arteries

12

The aorta branches into smaller arteries. Blood travels through these arteries into even smaller arteries in the body. The blood carries oxygen to all parts of the body.

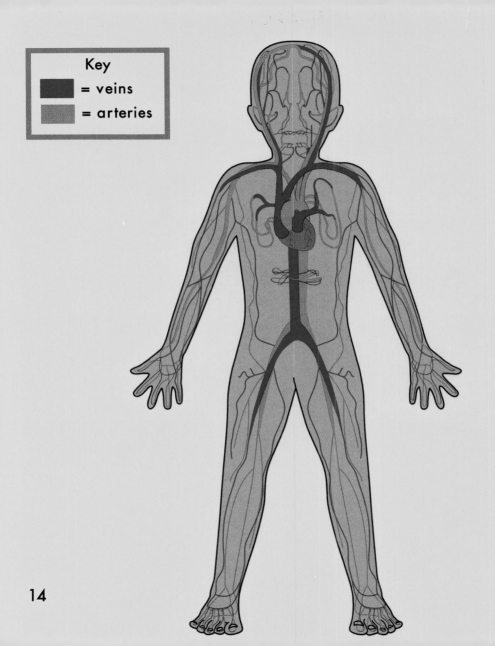

Key
■ = veins
■ = arteries

14

Veins are blood vessels
that carry blood back to
the heart. Blood that travels
through veins does not
carry oxygen.

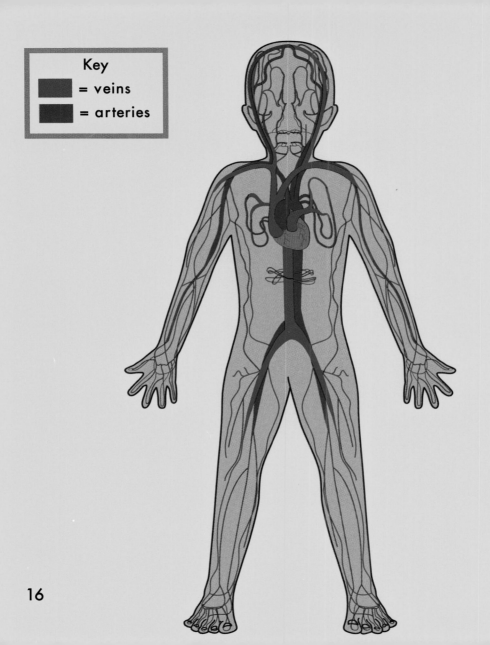

Key
■ = veins
■ = arteries

16

Blood travels back into the heart. The heart pumps the blood through the body again.

The heart pumps blood all the time. The heart keeps blood moving throughout the circulatory system.

The heart needs exercise to stay healthy.

Words to Know

aorta—the biggest artery in the body; the aorta carries blood away from the heart.

artery—a blood vessel that carries blood away from the heart; blood in arteries carries oxygen.

blood—the red liquid pumped through the body by the heart; an adult has about 1.5 gallons (5 liters) of blood.

blood vessel—a tube that carries blood around the body

heart—a body part inside the chest; the heart pumps blood all the time.

lung—a body part that takes air into and out of the body

oxygen—a gas found in the air; oxygen has no color or smell; all humans and animals need oxygen.

vein—a blood vessel that carries blood back to the heart; blood in veins does not carry oxygen.

Read More

Ballard, Carol. *The Heart and Circulatory System.* The Human Body. Austin, Texas: Raintree Steck-Vaughn, 1997.

Sandeman, Anna. *Blood.* Body Books. Brookfield, Conn.: Copper Beech Books, 1996.

Simon, Seymour. *The Heart: Our Circulatory System.* New York: Morrow Junior Books, 1996.

Stille, Darlene R. *The Circulatory System.* A True Book. New York: Children's Press, 1997.

Internet Sites

All about the Heart
http://kidshealth.org/kid/body/heart_noSW.html

Cardiovascular System
http://www.yucky.com/body/index.ssf?/systems/cardiovas/

The Heart
http://sln.fi.edu/biosci/biosci.html

The Life Pump: The Circulatory System
http://www.imcpl.lib.in.us/nov_circ.htm

Index/Word List

Word Count: 172
Early-Intervention Level: 17

Editorial Credits
Martha E. H. Rustad, editor; Kia Bielke, designer; Marilyn Moseley LaMantia,
Graphicstock, illustrator; Katy Kudela, photo researcher

Photo Credits
Bob Daemmrich/Pictor, 18
Jeff Myers/Pictor, 1
Jim Cummins/FPG International LLC, cover
Marilyn Moseley LaMantia, 4, 10
VCG/FPG International LLC, 20

The author thanks the children's section staff at the Allen County Public Library in
Fort Wayne, Indiana, for research assistance. The author also thanks Linda
Hathaway, CFCS, Health Educator, McMillen Center for Health Education, Fort
Wayne, Indiana.